Foreword

Your work with children is a ministry of profound importance and immeasurable impact. I know firsthand the importance of the church in providing children with a foundation of security, constructive activity, and a sense of being needed and valued in the sight of church members and of God.

As the granddaughter, daughter, and sister of Baptist ministers, I was taught that service was as essential as eating and sleeping and going to school. The church was the hub of black children's social existence, and caring black adults were buffers against the segregated and hostile outside world that told us we weren't important.

Children were taught—not by sermonizing but by personal example— that nothing was too lowly to do and that the work of our hands and the work of our minds were of equal dignity and value. I remember a debate my parents had about whether I was too young to go with an older brother to help clean the bed and bedsores of a very sick, poor woman. I went and learned early just how much the smallest helping hands and kindness can mean to a person in need.

The adults in our churches and community made children feel valued and important. They took time and paid attention to us. They struggled to find ways to keep us busy. While life was often hard and resources scarce, which is still the reality for so many today, we always knew who we were and that the measure of our worth was inside our heads and hearts and not outside in our possessions.

The legacies that parents and church and teachers left to my generation were priceless but not material: a living faith reflected in daily service, the discipline of hard work and perseverance, and a capacity to struggle in the face of adversity. They valued family life and family rituals and tried to be and expose us to good role models.

Today, children of every race and class in America need and deserve the same kind of loving support as was given to us by caring parents, preachers, teachers, churches, and communities. The more than 14 million poor children, as well as their middle-class and affluent counterparts, need to discover that their gifts are valued and used in the shared ministry of the church. All children should be helped to realize that their compassionate service with and for others is needed. All children should experience the welcome, love, and acceptance of congregation members. All children should feel that committed adults are speaking out for them, not only within the church but outside in the public policy arenas that so profoundly affect their lives.

Children As Partners in the Church offers an important glimpse into the changing world of children today and provides a valuable model of ministry with children that recognizes their gifts and perspectives as well as their needs. I hope that you will use it in your work with children.

I hope, too, that you will respond to the final chapter's call to faithful advocacy—to speak out on behalf of children in the church, community, nation, and world. Through your invaluable work ministering with children, you are better able than most to understand the varied needs of children and speak out for them so that all children receive the spiritual, emotional, physical, educational, and social support they need to develop their God-given potential. May God bless you in your ministry with children.

Marian Wright Edelman
Children's Defense Fund
May 1993

Contents

Children Today Speak Up

We are your children—
   children in your family,
     your church,
     your neighborhood;
   children you see every day,
     hear every day,
     speak to every day;
   children laughing and crying,
     playing and learning,
     watching and pretending.
We are your children, but
   do we see the same world as you,
     hear the same messages as you,
     speak the same language as you?
   Do we laugh and cry at the same things as you,
     play and learn in the same ways as you,
     watch and pretend as you?
We are your children.
   We see the world through eyes unfiltered by experience,
     hear the conflicting messages of the world,

speak our feelings through our behavior.
We are inquisitive and curious,
   sensitive and vulnerable,
   active and expressive.
We need models and positive examples,
   understanding and encouragement,
   security and love.
We are your children.
   See through our eyes.
   Hear our fears and hopes.
   Speak with us in love.

The World of Today's Children

When I was a child, my speech, my outlook, and my thoughts were all childish. When I grew up, I had finished with childish things (1 Corinthians 13:11, NEB).

Children today speak to us of the world as it appears to them and as it affects them. They are children, and they speak as children. They speak, but often we do not hear. Not only have we given up speaking as children speak, but we have also stopped listening to their ways of speaking. We see and hear only in part.

Today's children do not live in a secure world of fun and fantasy. They live with the reality of the world before them daily. They are continuously exposed to its harshness.

Today's children live in a world with a variety of family structures. Divorce has become more common over the past several years, resulting in more children living in nontraditional households. In some places divorce may be more the rule than the exception. In the third grade class taught by a friend of mine, only three of the twenty-nine children live with both of their parents. Other children live with one parent, grandparents, stepparents, foster parents, and, in one case, with an older sister and her husband.

How many times did your family move when you were a child? How many different schools did you attend during your elementary school years?

Families today are very mobile. The community our children have grown up in is considered very stable. Yet, in looking over our fifth grader's class picture, we discovered that of twenty-seven children, only thirteen have been in this school district since kindergarten. This would indicate that even within a stable rural community, fifty percent of the children have moved at least once during their elementary school years.

When were you first in a group with other children, other than church school? What was the purpose of the group?

Today's children are being placed in organized group situations more frequently and at an earlier age than in the past. Day-care centers and nursery schools have become an accepted part of the child's world, serving child-care needs as well as providing enrichment activities. A variety of organized groups are available for very young children. Swimming lessons for infants and exercise classes designed for children as young as one year are advertised. There are nursery schools that specialize in computer activities for three-year-olds. Dancing lessons begin with three-year-olds, and group music lessons for four-year-olds are not unusual.

Many children must be in group-care situations because their parents work either from necessity or by choice. Many children are in several group settings every day, possibly going from nursery school or babysitter to dance or music lessons. More children entering kindergarten today have had group experiences than previously was true in our society.

When do you recall becoming aware that there were differing values among people? At what age did you become aware of violence, murder, and war? Who were your childhood heroes and what values did they reflect?

The changes in family structure and the increased time young children spend in the care of persons other than their parents expose them to a variety of values. If we add to this the influence of television, particularly the heroes' involvement in violence, we can easily see why children may be confused about what is important. The value systems they see not only may differ from one another but probably actually conflict with one another.

Children today are part of a technological world. Cassette recorders (both audio and video), cameras, calculators, video games, and computers are all toys to today's children. These children are not intimidated by keyboards or flashing lights or questions presented by machines. They easily accept and use the technological wonders of our age.

These are some of the trends in the world of today's children. Not all children are affected by all of these changes, but all are probably affected by some of them.

Think of the children close to you. Which of the trends discussed affect you? affect the children? How do you respond to these influences in your life? How do the children respond? In what ways do your childhoods differ?

The Needs of Today's Children

Adults have socially and technologically changed the world in which today's children live and grow. The needs of children, however, remain much the same. Children still have physical, social-emotional, and intellectual needs and are dependent upon adults to help meet those needs.

Physical Needs

We can easily identify the physical needs of children: food, clothing, shelter, and a safe environment. However, we cannot assume that these needs are being met.

There are children in our society who suffer from hunger. There are even more children who are fed, but are nutritionally shortchanged. Research has shown that highly processed foods have detrimental effects, especially on children. The children's stamina, behavior, and ability to concentrate are all affected by the nutritional value of the foods they eat. Many children are allergic to the chemicals used to preserve and enhance foods today. These allergies often manifest themselves in behavior.

Children's clothing and shelter needs are met in varying degrees. There are children who lack clean clothing, jackets, shoes, and warm bedding. There are children who have more clothing than they need, and yet they feel that they must have certain brands or colors or styles. Advertising and peer pressure are very much a part of our children's lives, often making it difficult for them to distinguish between needs and wants.

Children need an environment that is safe and that takes into account their curious and adventuresome nature. Reasonable care needs to be taken to remove potential hazards, especially for very young children. All children have the right to be free from abuse. Some research has shown that sexual and physical abuse of children is much more common than most people believe. Frequently such abuse is committed by a family member or friend. The number of children being abused may or may not be increasing, but certainly the awareness and reporting of incidents of abuse are increasing. Physical abuse harms not only the child's body but his or her emotional and social growth as well.

Social-Emotional Needs

Love is the basic social-emotional need of all persons. Love must be expressed in specific ways to meet the needs of children as they grow and develop.

Children have the need for a sense of security. It is very difficult for them to feel secure when they are feeling deeply the impact of the separation and divorce of their parents or the tension due to a parent's unemployment, the family's financial problems, or the uncertain world situation. The force of these events can be lessened if a child feels the security that comes from receiving love and care. This sense of personal security and worth develops as the child is held and touched, talked with and listened to, and cared for tenderly.

Children need to be free to develop as unique persons who have a sense of self-worth. This requires acceptance, encouragement, and freedom from comparison with other children. Each child develops at her or his own pace and in individual ways, though each needs to experience every stage of the growth process. The young child needs to take the first steps toward independence by responding with an emphatic "No!" as a two-year-old does. The four-year-old exclaiming, "I want to do it myself!" is taking a further step toward independence. In the early elementary school years, ages five through seven, the child needs to identify with an adult of the same sex. This role model may be parent, teacher, or other significant adult. As the child approaches the middle elementary years, the need to be part of a group becomes apparent. The child needs to put the good of the group before his or her own wishes, to follow the rules, and to conform.

Children today need strong adult models who express their values in everyday life and can talk about those values and how they affect their decisions and actions. Children need this kind of help to sort out the variety of lifestyles and values that they see every day. They need to know that values and how they are applied reflect a choice. They need to be given chances to make decisions in a safe and accepting atmosphere in order for them to understand that decisions have consequences. All this requires intentional effort from the adults who relate to children.

Intellectual Needs

Children also have intellectual needs. The development of intellectual skills depends upon the child being exposed to a variety of experiences and having the freedom to explore what these experiences have to offer. Children need to use all their senses to discover and learn about the world around them. They need to see, to hear, to touch, to smell, and to taste.

Children need to be free to develop interests and skills without the pressure of being pushed. They need time to reflect upon and to find value in their experiences by talking about them and naming them. Reflection is necessary if an activity is to have meaning for the child.

The Hopes of Our Children

The hopes of children reflect their world. In recalling our own childhood hopes, we found that they were in three areas: friends, family, and future. When we were children, these were some of our hopes. With regard to our friends, we recall—
- hoping to be liked by others.
- hoping to be chosen for sports teams.
- hoping to be accepted in the "in groups."
- hoping to be able to spend time with friends.

When we think of family, we remember—
- hoping that Father's new job would be permanent.
- hoping that our extended families—including aunts, uncles, and cousins—would continue to be nearby and that we would all remain close.
- hoping to please adult family members.

Our hopes for the future included—
- hoping that the air-raid procedures we practiced would never be necessary.
- hoping to be accepted for what we were and not because we belonged to a certain racial or ethnic group.
- hoping that polio would not strike us or our friends.
- hoping that the new technology and scientific discoveries would solve the problems of the world.

What hopes do you recall from your childhood? How do these reflect your fears? your living situation?

Today's children are living in a world that is very different from the world of our childhood. Life was simpler then, and our overall hope was that life was going to continue as it was. Today's children feel some of the same pressures we felt but have additional pressures as well. Children see, hear, and often participate vicariously in crime, violence, death, and nuclear destruction through television and movies.

They have few buffers to shield them from the harshness of the world today. Except for infancy, today's children may not have a time of real innocence, a world of childhood.

What are the hopes of children living and growing in this kind of world? Some of their hopes are the same as those we recalled. Others' hopes reflect their world of today. With regard to friends, children today—

- hope to be liked by others, to be popular.
- hope to be chosen for teams.
- hope to be liked because they wear the right clothes and have the right hair style.
- hope to be liked in spite of differences of language or skin color.

Children also have hopes for their families. They—

- hope their families will stay together (not just their extended families but their primary families of parents and children); they hope their parents will not separate or divorce.
- hope that their parents will get back together, if separation and divorce are part of their lives.
- hope that they will still be loved and accepted when their divorced parents remarry.
- hope to please parents, grandparents, and other loved adults.
- hope for security for their families when they feel the stress caused by job losses and financial problems.

When thinking of the future, today's children—

- hope that adults will not use the power of science and technology for destruction.
- hope that nuclear war will not be allowed to happen.

We are living in the future that we had great hopes for as children. It did not all turn out as we hoped. Science and technology have not solved the world's problems. We no longer practice air-raid drills, since the procedure would be useless in light of the power of today's weapons. We no longer worry about polio, but leukemia and other forms of cancer seem more common among children. We hoped for life to continue as it was; children today hope for life to continue.

Adult Leaders
with Children Speak Up

There are different kinds of spiritual gifts, but the same Spirit gives them. There are different ways of serving, but the same Lord is served. There are different abilities to perform service, but the same God gives ability to everyone for their particular service (1 Corinthians 12:4-6).

We are adults who work with children. We give our time, energy, skills, and often our money for this task because we sense God's call to minister with children. We are mostly volunteers with many other demands upon us. Our world affects how we work with children.

Our World

Our adult world is lived in various settings: big cities, suburban towns, and rural communites. We live in a variety of family situations. Some of us are single, others married; some have children in our homes, others do not; some of us live alone, some with other adults. We relate to children in several ways: as parents, school teachers, church school teachers, scout or other group leaders, aunts and uncles, grandparents, and friends. We range in age from young to old, in teaching experience from novice to old hand, and in education from grade school to graduate level. There is variation in our Christian experience, our skills and talents, and our financial resources.

We are very different from one another, for each of us is God's unique creation, growing through a special set of experiences. Yet there is much we have in common.

What is the world like for us as leaders of children?

We find that calls for our time come from many directions. We have homes to maintain and families to care for; we have jobs to do and any number of organizations to support; we have classes to take and hobbies and other interests to pursue. We take time to read books, watch television programs, and attend sporting or entertainment events. We need time to cultivate friendships and stay in touch with our extended families. We feel that there is often very little time left to spend in preparation for our scheduled times with children. This is not to say that we think these times are unimportant or that we are not committed to children. We do want to be with them in meaningful ways. We know the importance of significant adults in their lives. But our world is moving and changing rapidly, and we often get caught up in the urgent at the expense of the important. We sometimes have trouble giving children the priority they need and deserve.

Many of us are uncomfortable with the rapid changes in today's world. We are amazed at the ease with which children accept and use video equipment, computers, and other technological wonders that just a few years ago were the stuff of science fiction. We sometimes find the changes in society difficult to accept and unsettling to our sense of security.

Many times we find the world increasingly complex, so that making choices and decisions is more difficult. Determining our moral responsibility is often confusing in such a pluralistic and fast-changing society. We can understand children's confusion when we too become aware of the amount of violence and unethical behavior in our world.

Reflect on how your world is related to your work with children. What experiences have led you into working with children? How does the community in which you live affect your work with them? How do the demands on your time affect your relationships with children? How do you respond to social and technological change?

Our Needs

We have many of the same needs as children. Much of our time and energy is spent in meeting the physical needs of ourselves and our family members.

We also need security. For many of us, our personal security is shaken by a break in a personal relationship caused by separation, divorce, or the death of a loved one. Our personal and financial security may be shaken by a job loss.

We also have needs related to being adult leaders working with children. We need training for the job that we are expected to do with children.

This training should include knowledge of the characteristics and primary concerns of the group's age level. Valuable skills for working with children involve learning how to incorporate various teaching methods and techniques for planning and evaluating our time with the children. Learning to share our faith effectively with children should be an integral part of our training.

We also need support from members of the congregation as we work with children. Their support may include providing us with adequate space and materials, financial backing, reliable substitutes, supportive pastors, and recognition of the fact that working with children is important. In return, we should share with others what God is doing in our lives through our contacts with children.

We need opportunities to grow. Interacting with others who share in the ministry with children gives us an opportunity to share ideas and to encourage and be encouraged by one another. We should have opportunities to grow as adults of faith and to share with other adults in worship, study, and personal support.

Sometimes this may mean that we do not have primary responsibility for a group of children for a semester or a year.

What needs do you feel at this time as you work with children? How can those needs be met? What steps are you taking to meet those needs?

Our Hopes and Expectations

We work with children because we care about them. This means that we have hopes for their present and their future. We also have hopes and expectations for ourselves as we relate to children.

When we work with children in the church, we hope that the other adult members will show an interest in the children's ministry by accepting each child, seeing children as part of the total congregation and acknowledging that children have valid gifts for ministering to and with adults.

We hope—

- that the adult members will rejoice in the growth of the children among them.

- that the children will find, within the adult membership, persons who exemplify the values we are trying to teach.
- that parents will support and participate in the Christian nurture of their children.
- that the children will be valued as persons of worth at home.
- that we can make a difference in the world by making a difference in the life of each child.
- that we can help to prepare each child to make a difference in the world.
- that each child will come to know Christ and to live the fullness that such a life promises.

What other hopes and expectations do you have in your ministry with children? What hopes do you have for each child with whom you work? What hopes and expectations do you have for yourself in your relationships with children?

Nurtured as Partners in Ministry

"There is a boy here who has five loaves of barley bread and two fish. But they will certainly not be enough for all these people."

"Make the people sit down," Jesus told them. (There was a lot of grass there.) So all the people sat down; there were about five thousand men. Jesus took the bread, gave thanks to God, and distributed it to the people who were sitting there. He did the same with the fish, and they all had as much as they wanted (John 6:9-11).

Children and adults are in partnership. Partnership can be a reality when we realize that all people are of value in the eyes of God and that all of us are growing, changing persons in the act of becoming. Growing and becoming requires nurture, and children and adults have much to offer each other.

The Gifts That Each Brings

A young boy shared his lunch with Jesus. Picture the child. He overheard the discussion of the disciples. Timidly he said, "I have some food," and he held out his small lunch. The adults may have had food, but they did not offer it. The true gift of the child was his willingness to share what he had. Jesus, using his gifts and the gift of the child, ministered to the crowd. The gifts of both were needed.

Children and adults can nurture one another and minister to others as they share gifts. Children give us the gift of trust. They place themselves in our hands. This is a tremendous responsibility, but it is what we ask for when we seek to teach them, to lead them, and to minister with them.

Children give us a fresh point of view. They come to each new situation with few preconceptions. Their imagination, wonder, spontaneity, and excitement reflect their openness. Their approach to life is an example of their faith.

Children bring their unrestrained emotions to encounters with adults. They express their anger and delight, disappointment and pleasure. They express their emotions with a hug or by reaching for your hand.

These gifts that children share with us show us the elements of faith. They remind us that trust and dependence, our view of God and the world, and our response to God are what faith is all about. John Westerhoff states it in this way: "We adults need to be born again. We adults need to be converted to new ways of perceiving. We adults need to be encouraged to open ourselves to radically new experiences of God. And our children can help us!"[1]

Think about the children you relate to. What gifts have you recently received from them? How can you encourage them to share their gifts with others?

Adults who are partners with children also have gifts to share. One of the most important is the gift of acceptance. Every child needs someone to listen to events that have happened at home, to jokes and riddles, to fears and triumphs. Every child needs someone to listen to his or her questions sensitively.

Each adult has a faith story that is his or her own. Each person has had a different journey to God. Sharing honestly at the child's level of understanding can be important. The child can come to know that God continues to work in the lives of people, even through the ups and downs. When adults share their faith stories with children in the context of the church, children will see that the church community and a personal relationship with God is important for encouragement and renewal.

Adults can also share the gift of experience, the truths of the Bible, and the wisdom of the church through the ages. We have evaluated what has been successful and what has failed and have determined the easy ways of doing things and the ways that are more difficult. Our

[1] John H. Westerhoff III, *Bringing Up Children in the Christian Faith* (Minneapolis: Winston Press, Inc., 1980), p. 23.

experience is most valuable when it is used in conjunction with the spontaneity and creativity of children. Our experience may have shown us several ways of doing things, but there are still other ways that will be visible only to a child!

Each person has unique gifts to share with children. Some people have great patience; some can tell stories well. What are the gifts that you have shared with children? What gifts do you have that have been hidden? How can you share these hidden gifts?

Children and Adults as Growing Persons

And Jesus increased in wisdom and stature, and in favor with God and man (Luke 2:52).

Though there are differences between adults and children, there is also much that they have in common. All persons are children of God and, as such, exhibit one of the most obvious characteristics of children. We are all growing. As Jesus grew—intellectually, physically, spiritually, and socially—so do we. None of these types of growth occurs independently of the others; all are intertwined. Theories of development have been proposed to describe growth in all these areas. Though theorists chart patterns of growth, they are careful to offer some cautions when considering these patterns. Each person is an individual, unique from all others. No persons will fit the theories exactly. Each person develops at his or her own pace. Each stage is necessary and right for the individual at a particular time in life.

The growth theories reflect what we can expect of persons of certain ages. It is important for adults who work with children to understand the probable stages of development of the children with whom they relate. This will help them to plan appropriate activities, to be understanding of individual differences, and to accept children as they are.

Chart A shows the physical, social-emotional, and intellectual growth patterns of children.

The Development of Faith

Faith, too, follows a developmental process that is related to the other processes of development. Children are persons of faith. Their faith may be different from the faith of an adult, but it is real and genuine and fits the development and needs of the child. Faith involves building trust, developing a body of beliefs, and taking action on those beliefs.

Building trust is the major task of infancy and early childhood. Trust

CHART A[2]

	NURSERY Birth–1	NURSERY 2–3 years	KINDERGARTEN 4–5 years	PRIMARY Grades 1–2	MIDDLER Grades 3–4	JUNIOR Grades 5–6
PHYSICAL DEVELOPMENT	Crawls	Talks Walks / Exercises bladder control	Develops large muscles	Develops small muscles and eye-hand coordination		
SOCIAL-EMOTIONAL DEVELOPMENT	Trusts	Demonstrates independence		Identifies with parent of same sex	Conforms to group ideas, goals, etc.	
INTELLECTUAL DEVELOPMENT		Is self-centered / Senses and recognizes experiences / Can't relate one fact to another / Can't check whether or not mistaken		Is less self-centered / Thinks concretely / Sometimes makes generalizations / Sometimes checks conclusions		Is other-centered / Thinks abstractly / Makes generalizations / Checks conclusions

[2]Linda Isham, *On Behalf of Children* (Valley Forge: Judson Press, 1975), p. 16.

develops as the infant is cared for. If the needs of the child are met with love, the baby will come to trust the ones who meet those needs. The infant first attaches trust to parents, especially the mother or the primary caregiver. Over a period of time and with the encouragement of parents, that trust is expanded to include others.

Mistrust or fear is also developed during infancy. If a child's needs are met with hostility and anger, the child learns fear. If they are met with neglect, the child learns mistrust. If a parent is anxious, the child will sense that all is not well.

Preelementary children are still extending their trust. Their faith can be nurtured at this age if they are helped to extend their trust to the people of God. Their trust will be extended if they are accepted with love and care.

Young children are taking the first steps toward building a body of beliefs when they learn to attach words to things. They are learning to communicate with speech, to name objects and ideas, and to make their needs and wants known to others. They use their new skill to ask questions, often beginning, ''Why . . .?'' They can begin to understand God in relationship to their own experiences. They can understand that God loves and cares for them as their parents do. They are able to understand God as the Creator of the wonders of nature that they see, touch, taste, smell, and hear.

Young children begin to discover that they are separate beings, that they can act independently of their parents. They can decide what they want or what they will do. The development of independence is necessary if one is to develop an owned set of beliefs and if one is to act on those beliefs. This process begins in the preelementary years.

Children of early elementary age are expanding their world. They are building trust in teachers and friends. They understand that Jesus was a real person. They trust Jesus because they have been introduced to him through people they trust. They are aware of God as the Creator. Many children feel they can talk freely to God. They think in terms of actual people or events that belong to their immediate experience but can also relate some Bible stories to their own lives.

Children in early elementary years are becoming more aware of others. As concrete thinkers they see the adult Jesus as a teacher who had a special relationship with God. They can understand that the church continues the work of Jesus by helping people to live the way God wants them to live.

Children of older elementary age are becoming more independent. Friends are very important and influential in their lives. Many of them begin to question the faith of their parents, especially if they feel forced or if their experiences with the church family are unpleasant. They make choices about what they want to learn or how they will participate. They enjoy belonging to groups and can cooperate in activities that they enjoy.

Children are continuously growing in trust, developing their beliefs, and discovering that they can act independently. Their faith is one of belonging, of being part of the family of God and a particular community of worship. They observe and imitate those persons of faith, including Jesus, who are important in their lives. They are developing a body of beliefs as they recognize God as the source of life and Jesus as a person who showed us how to live. They want to act on their faith and serve God by helping others. They want to belong to the community of faith.

Think about the children you know. How do they exhibit trust? What beliefs do they hold? How do they put their beliefs into action? How do they express their desire to belong to the faith community?

Recall your own faith development. How does the faith development process outlined here compare with your own childhood experience?

The Faith of Youth and Adulthood

Youth is a time of great change. Physically young people are changing rapidly. Their intellectual abilities are expanding. Their social relationships are very important to them and lead them into contact with people of many different beliefs. Faith often goes through change as a result of the quest for independence and self-definition and for the answer to the lifelong question "Who am I?" Youth seek to discover whether their trust in God and in the faith community has been well placed. They question their beliefs, measuring them against the beliefs of others and testing them in the world outside of the church. They question the importance of acting on their own beliefs as opposed to accepting the prevailing behaviors of people their age.

The development of faith does not stop when one becomes an adult. Though many adults develop a faith of their own, they are repeatedly reevaluating their trust in God and the faith community as they go through crises in their lives. They refine their beliefs as they are challenged by new ideas and experiences. Adults act on their beliefs with different degrees of trust at different times and in different situations. An adult faith is one that is open to reevaluation in light of new insights. It is a growing faith.

Consider your faith development throughout your youth and into adulthood. What events of significance stand out for you? How would you describe your present growth and development? How can seeing yourself as a growing person help you in your relationship with children?

Lifestyles of the Community of Faith

Each community of faith has its own personality, growing out of its history. Some communities of faith emphasize family spirit, some Bible study, and some missions and service to the community. Whatever the personality or emphasis of the faith community, there are some characteristics that will allow for maximum growth of its members, children, youth, and adults.

Describe your community of faith. What characteristics do you see there that encourage growth and lead children toward a life of faith? What do you see that hinders the children's growth of faith?

Acceptance will be characteristic of the community that is living by faith. The congregation will include those who are seeking to live their beliefs in faith. It will include those in need of food or clothing, in need of education or employment, or in need of forgiveness or reassurance. There will be those who are just beginning to build their beliefs and those who have lived with and refined their beliefs over many years. Persons of all ages, each one appreciating the others as children of God, will be included within the community of faith.

The community of faith will be a growing community. We often think of growth in terms of increasing numbers, but we are referring to the growth of the spirit. Members of this community will be expanding their capacity to trust, expanding their beliefs, and acting on their beliefs individually and as a community. Trust can be expanded through age-group experiences, beliefs refined through study and discussion, and action taken in the mission of the church.

Living by example will be characteristic of the faith community. Adults are aware that children follow their example and strive to be worthy of imitation. The community will be an example to those around it, an example of love and care. The children will set an example of openness and excitement for the adults.

The community of faith will be intergenerational. All age groups will relate to one another. Westerhoff explains that three generations are necessary in the faith community. Children, the first generation, can be persons of vision. The second generation confronts the community with reality. The third generation provides memory and a sense of continuity. All three are necessary because each makes its own contributions.[3]

Why a Ministry of Partnership?

We want to be in partnership with children because it is the most effective way to teach them. Our purpose is to help them grow in Christian faith.

We need to be in partnership with children for our own growth in faith. Children are capable of learning and teaching, of receiving and giving, and being challenged and of challenging. We want to be in partnership with children so that we do not lose sight of our status as children of God. Children remind us of the need to be open and active in response to God.

What goals would you set for children in a partnership ministry?
What goals would you set for yourself?

Adults and children can nurture one another as they share their gifts. Children need our understanding and acceptance; we need their spontaneity and imagination. They can learn by listening to our faith stories. We can learn by listening to the children. We have a ministry to one another and a ministry as partners. In partnership we can use our strengths to witness to God's love in the world.

[3] John H. Westerhoff III, *Will Our Children Have Faith?* (New York: The Seabury Press, Inc., 1976), p. 53.

The Church School

"Israel, remember this! The LORD—and the LORD alone—is our God. Love the LORD your God with all your heart, with all your soul, and with all your strength. Never forget these commands that I am giving you today. Teach them to your children. Repeat them when you are at home and when you are away, when you are resting and when you are working. Tie them on your arms and wear them on your foreheads as a reminder. Write them on the doorposts of your houses and on your gates" (Deuteronomy 6:4-9).

Most church members feel that it is important to have a church school, especially for children and youth. They expect the church school to teach the Bible, draw children and their families into the church, clarify and strengthen Christian values, and provide peer groups for their children. Some of these expectations may be challenged by the purpose of the church school and by what we know about the development of individuals.

What are your expectations for the church school? What do you think are the expectations of the members of your church? How do these expectations take into consideration the developmental stages of the persons involved?

The Purpose of the Church School

The objective of the church's educational ministry is that all persons be aware of God through God's self-disclosure,
especially God's redeeming love as revealed in Jesus Christ,
and,
enabled by the Holy Spirit, respond in faith and love;
that
as new persons in Christ they may
knowwho they are and what their human situation means,
grow as children of God rooted in the Christian community,
live in obedience to the will of God in every relationship,
fulfill their common vocation in the world,
and
abide in the Christian hope.[1]

These goals describe a lifelong process of growth and renewal. Each person—adult, youth, or child—will grow toward this goal in ways that are appropriate to his or her stage of development. As each person grows and changes, the goals will be achieved again and again with new understanding. For example, a child and an adult may both be aware of God, and yet their levels of awareness will be very different. Each level is valid for that person at that time.

When we understand the objectives of Christian education as a lifelong process, we are freed from the pressure to teach concepts that are beyond the understanding of those with whom we are working. We are free to accept each as an individual who is growing at a unique pace. We can relax in the knowledge that each child will encounter the gospel again and again and respond in new ways each time. We can realize that we too are growing. We do not have to have final answers, for we are not finished with learning.

Since these goals are long-term and general, we need to develop specific objectives for our ministry with children in the church school. We need clear statements of what we hope to achieve. These objectives should be achievable, based on the needs of the children and on their levels of skill and understanding. Such objectives can help us maintain a sense of purpose and can be guidelines for evaluating our sessions with children.

We can consider the following objective as an example: By the end of the church school year, the four-year-old children will recognize the Bible as the source of stories about Jesus and God.

---

[1]*Foundations for Curriculum* (Valley Forge: Educational Ministries, ABC/USA, 1966), p. 13.

- Is this objective based on the needs and probable developmental levels of the children involved?
- Is it compatible with the expectations of the teachers, parents, and other members of the congregation?
- Is it achievable?

Think about what you hope to achieve in the lives of the children with whom you work in the church school. What are some of your objectives for accomplishing this purpose? Do your objectives meet the above criteria? If you have no stated objectives, develop some using these criteria as guidelines.

The Church School

Most church members think of church school in terms of a teacher imparting knowledge in a classroom setting and using books, pencils, and paper to teach children who are sitting and responding to his or her questions. This image implies that adults have all the answers, that Christian faith can be taught/learned through the transmission of ideas, facts, or concepts, and that children are basically receptive participants in the learning process.

How does this description of church school fit with your own childhood church school experience? How does it fit with what you know of how children learn and grow? How does it fit with what we want to accomplish with children as partners?

When we reflect on our experiences as children in church school, we may remember teachers who made us feel special by giving us responsibilities, by relating to us outside the classroom, by being real persons to us. We may remember other students with whom we played, explored ideas, and worked. Perhaps we recall classrooms only in relation to what we were doing in them. Probably we do not recall curriculum materials or what was said during times when we had to sit and listen. We may remember when teachers spoke just to us as individuals. Our experiences tell us that this classroom model is not enough. When adults stepped outside of the traditional mold, they had the most influence in our lives.

Recognizing that the church school is still a primary Christian education effort, we need to apply to the church school situation what we know of how children learn and develop in faith. Therefore, we would like to challenge you to implement some of these ideas in the church school. The church school can be a place for experimenting, for exploring, and for trying activities and ideas to see how they relate to life. It can be a place for physical involvement and reflection.

So what does this image of the church school mean? The teacher must be a *planner*. Sessions in church school do have structure and content. The teacher must plan for the use of time and space and materials. This includes selecting and presenting content. It means planning to use various ways to present the content so that the learners can interact with it in many different ways.

The teacher is an *interpreter*. The teacher interprets the Bible and the curriculum resources. In the process of interpreting the content, the teacher may have to adapt the resources. The teacher's awareness of how the children will understand the content is vital. This helps the teacher decide on appropriate content and methods to use in interpreting it to the children.

The teacher is a *resource person*. The teacher's experience, knowledge, and loving concern can be shared with children. The teacher's contribution as a resource person is not merely to give answers or offer information but also to assist the children in seeking answers. "Let's look together!" opens the door for discovery and discussion. An honest "I don't know; perhaps we can find out together" says to the children that it is okay not to know all the answers all the time and that seeking is encouraged.

The teacher is a *helper*. The teacher is aware of children as whole persons with knowledge, thinking ability, feelings, family and social relationships, and a need for physical participation. The teacher accepts the whole child, uses methods that allow the whole child to interact with the gospel, provides materials and experiences that stimulate the child, and assists the child to reflect on the meanings of his or her own life.

The teacher is a *participant*. This may be a role the teacher has not assumed in the classroom model. As a participant the adult is not always the authority. This means responding to questions or in discussion with statements such as "I believe . . ." or "I feel. . . ." Such responses allow for the child to consider the statements and to develop his or her own beliefs and feelings. In activities the teacher listens to the suggestions offered by the children, and they all try them out together.

As a participant the teacher is a *model*. The teacher models acceptance, respect for individuals, nurturing behavior, and how to make a contribution. The teacher creates the atmosphere for mutual encouragement and growth.

What other roles do you see for the teacher? Would adopting these roles change your teaching style? How would this type of church school atmosphere affect the lives of children?

In this type of setting, children are no longer expected to be passive recipients of information. They assume different roles.

Children are *active participants*. They move freely about the room, talking and sharing with others. They are involved individually and together in activities. They share in discussions and discoveries. They bring their whole persons to the class session.

Children are *decision makers*. They help decide on rules and standards for the group. They offer suggestions and help evaluate possible activities. They help choose which activities they will participate in and which they will not. As they participate in the decision-making process, they will increase in the skills of making decisions.

Children are *contributors*. Every member of the group has a responsibility for the life of the group. Each child has resources, skills and talents, suggestions, and a unique outlook to contribute to the life of the group. As contributions are accepted, the children grow in self-esteem and trust within the group.

Children are *seekers*. They want to learn, to explore, to try things. In their early years they will touch, taste, and smell all they see. They will ask questions. They want to know "why" and "how."

Children are *teachers/learners*. They are learning to trust and teach others about trust as they learn to be trustworthy. They learn facts and concepts, and they teach as they help others to understand these facts and concepts. In the give and take of exploring ways to act on their beliefs, they are teaching *and* learning appropriate behavior.

Children are *members of a partnership*. They share the responsibility for their own growth with adults. They contribute to the growth of others by sharing themselves.

These roles will be lived out differently at different ages and stages of growth. In most church schools, the children are divided into age groups. Let's look at each age group and see how the roles of adults and children together might be carried out.

How many of these roles do the children in your class assume? How does assuming some of these roles change the children's self-concept or their attitude about church school?

The Nursery—Developing Trust

For the very young child, the development of faith is largely involved with developing trust. The child is an active participant in this process. Trust in God will grow out of trust in the people of God. The child in the church school nursery needs to feel, "I am cared for. My needs will be met. I am loved." In this way the child is learning to trust. Adults who work with very young children are acting on their belief that each one is a child of God and worthy of love and acceptance.

What do these adults do to nurture trust in the infant? To help in the development of trust, they meet the needs of the young child in a caring way. They express love in their words, tone of voice, and manner. They become a consistent, dependable part of the young child's life.

We sometimes hear that anyone can take care of the nursery. Considering the importance of this stage in the development of faith, we want people with genuine love for young children to care for them in the church school nursery.

Even in the nursery we can have a partnership with the children. What can an infant contribute to the partnership? Infants are teachers, reminding us of the miracle of the gift of life, of the great promise that every child of God holds, and of the change and growth that are the essence of life. They teach us patience, humility, and joy in the simple things. They renew feelings of tenderness and warmth as they snuggle against a shoulder, hold tightly to a finger, or give a first smile of recognition.

Preelementary—A Sense of Self

The preelementary years are truly years of exploration and discovery! The teacher can plan for the children's active participation by organizing the room with a variety of interest centers or areas. During a session there can be time and space for children to explore their physical limits, including running and jumping and climbing; puzzles with a few large pieces; crayons, paints, and play dough; stories to hear and songs to sing (many of them with actions, for actions give meaning to the words); pictures and books to look at; a building area with blocks and cars; a homeliving area with dolls and dishes; and a dress-up area with both men's and women's clothing. All of these contribute to a child's development as a seeker and decision maker. All of these can help children explore life in a safe atmosphere, discovering things about themselves and their world.

It is most important that the room have adults of faith who share with the children. How do these adults relate to young children in order to help them expand their trust and begin to build concepts necessary for forming Christian beliefs? They lovingly continue to meet the needs of the children, letting go as the children become increasingly able to meet their own needs. Adults working with young children offer help when it is needed and yet leave plenty of room for "I can do it myself!" They encourage children to develop a sense of their own capabilities.

Teachers of young children should help them develop the concept of the worth of the individual, the idea that each person is a child of God. They can do this by treating each child with the respect due a child of God. They speak to children at the eye level of each child. This may mean sitting on the floor or on a small chair or kneeling so that their eyes are level with those of the child. They call each child by his or her name. When a child is absent from the group, the adults call it to the attention of the other children, expressing that the absent one is missed. During times of prayer children who are ill or away are remembered. Children and adults together celebrate birthdays and special events in the life of each child.

Adults help young children become aware of God as the Creator when they discover the natural world with the children. As the children explore the wonders of nature with adults, adults may verbally recognize God as the source. "Thank you, God, for the flowers." "Sunshine helps the flowers grow. Why else did God give us sunshine?" Such comments and questions growing out of experiences with the children will help them come to know God as the Creator.

Adults should begin to acquaint the children with Jesus. Stories of the baby Jesus, of Jesus as a child, and of Jesus as a man of kindness will be meaningful to children of this age.

Adults will help young children to identify the Bible as an important book when they keep the Bible in evidence in the room. When sharing Bible stories with the children, the teacher can identify the Bible as the source of the stories. When curriculum resources for the session use a short verse, the teacher can look it up with the children and read it from the Bible. The teacher can share that the Bible is a resource and tells us about God and how God wants us to love and care for one another. The adults can model and encourage this kind of relationship.

Young children in partnership with adults contribute curiosity, excitement, and a sense of wonder. As seekers, they contribute questions that cause adults to think through their own faith in simple terms. They bring the fun of exploring language and meaning, of uninhibited play, and of trying new things. They invite caring adults to join them.

Early Elementary—An Expanding World

The atmosphere for early elementary children is one of exploring. Exploration requires active participation and the contribution of ideas and discoveries. All this implies movement, and the teacher must plan for this in the room arrangement, the variety of activities, and in the use of time.

Many teachers are using learning centers with early elementary children. Learning centers may certainly be one way of structuring a session, at least in part. The centers need to be set up for maximum participation and aimed toward success experiences for the children. Learning centers cannot stand on their own, however. The children need time in each session to share with each other and with adults. There needs to be intentional contact between the teacher and each child. The teachers need to be immediately available to the children for clarification, shared thoughts, and conversation.

Learning centers can allow for practice in making choices, in going at one's own pace, and in interacting in small groups. However, they are not the answer in every situation. Learning centers may be frustrating when a group is very small because they tend to divide children into solitary activities. If learning centers are not encouraging the children to interact with one another, the materials, and the gospel as it applies to their lives, then they are not meeting their purpose. The structure of the class should provide for the growth of faith by providing a trusting atmosphere, content and experiences for forming beliefs, and opportunities to act on those beliefs.

In the setting for early elementary children, teachers will continue to introduce them to Jesus through stories from the Bible. The children can understand that Jesus was a real person as they hear about his involvement with people in everyday situations. They recognize Jesus as a teacher.

Teachers with early elementary children will plan opportunities for them to use their developing reading skills by using the Bible. Helping the children to find a Scripture passage and follow it in their Bibles as it is read by one who wants to read should grow easily out of the time of discussion and storytelling. Using the Bible in such a way can help the children to increase in skill and can affirm their growing abilities. It will let them know that the teacher feels the Bible is important.

Adults can help children of early elementary age begin to act on the belief that we are called to serve others. Children and adults can be involved together in simple, short-term projects. For example, during church school time small gifts or cards can be made to share with shut-ins. Then the children and adults together can take the gifts, spending time visiting with people who may be lonely. After you have done this, discussion can help the children to identify the value of the experience.

When they talk about how they felt and how they think the person they visited might have felt, they can recognize the importance of serving others even in small ways. "This, then, is what I command you: love one another" (John 15:17).

During the elementary years peer groups become very important. Adults can help the children to become caring groups. By functioning as guides, participants, and models, teachers can create an atmosphere of love and acceptance that will allow the children to experience a caring relationship with one another.

Children of early elementary age have much to contribute to a partnership with adults in the church school. They contribute enthusiasm and energy and joy in learning. They also contribute a mirror for adults. They imitate the behavior of adults, and thus give adults a new view of themselves. They contribute a sensitivity to those who are in need of help and can raise the awareness of adults who will listen. They remind us of the importance of friendships in our lives as we see the children develop strong bonds with their peers.

Later Elementary

Older elementary children are better able to read and write and express themselves than their younger brothers and sisters. They have developed and are developing many talents and interests that they would like to share. A church school could help these children explore the Christian life in an atmosphere of understanding and support.

There are many ways in which children of this age can share as partners in the church school. They can be partners with adults in setting rules and standards. A discussion of the kind of group in which they feel comfortable and how they like to be treated will give guidelines for standards. The children can organize these ideas into standards of behavior for the group. The children will accept greater responsibility for their own behavior if they have some input into the rules they are expected to follow. As time passes, the standards may need to be reviewed and revised. Questions such as, "Are these rules still what we want? Have we left anything out? If they are not working, why not? What do we need to change, or do we just need to be reminded?" will stimulate evaluation of the standards and of behavior.

Planning is an important part of partnership between adults and later elementary children. At the beginning of a unit, such questions as "What do we already know about this subject? What would you like to know more about?" can give the teacher insight into the children and will let the children know that they are respected as thinking people. In planning with the children, the teacher can offer suggestions of activities and accept the childen's suggestions. Then, together, they can make decisions about which activities to use and the order in which to use them. Seeking and using the children's suggestions will encourage their creativity and interest. Evaluation is a part of the planning process. As the sessions proceed, ask, "Are we learning what we wanted to learn? If not, what do we need to change?" At the end of a unit, ask questions like "What did you learn during this unit? What activity did you like best and why? What can we do about what we have learned?" The teacher can use these learnings to plan for later sessions, to develop projects, and to challenge personal action.

Learning centers can be used with older elementary children. They can contain more written information than would be used for younger children. However, even these older children still learn best by active participation. Some centers may contain pencil-and-paper activities, but there also need to be art activities, music, projects, research, and other suggestions the children may have.

Children of later elementary age are very conscious of their peers. Involvement in activities and projects as a group can be important to them. They can contribute a spirit of enthusiasm to the entire congregation as they attack projects such as pulling weeds around the church or earning money for a food pantry. Adults can help these children develop characteristics of loyalty, enthusiasm, and a sense of justice as they help them step beyond the church school session and into the world.

Older elementary children and adults have much to contribute to one another. Many children of this age are seeking adults who will serve as role models and with whom they can develop relationships. Adults who respond may become very significant in the lives of these young people.

In partnership with adults children may contribute their concern for others and their desire to take action. They contribute questions of increasing complexity and present fresh insight into biblical truths as they begin to grasp some abstract ideas.

Intergenerational Classes—Children and Adults Together

Children and adults have much to learn from one another. Intergenerational classes are another possible way to be partners in the church school. Such classes may be held on a periodic basis, such as during Advent, during Lent, or for special occasions such as a church anniversary or a mission study. These sessions should be activity centered so that all may participate, with structured time for reflection and sharing. Such a time could be organized by using learning centers, perhaps with the stipulation that children and adults work together. It might be organized by family groupings or ''adopted'' families. The important thing is to mix the generations.

Corporate Worship: All God's Children Gather

> Some people brought children to Jesus for him to place his hands on them, but the disciples scolded the people. When Jesus noticed this, he was angry and said to his disciples, "Let the children come to me, and do not stop them, because the Kingdom of God belongs to such as these. I assure you that whoever does not receive the Kingdom of God like a child will never enter it."
> Then he took the children in his arms, placed his hands on each of them, and blessed them (Mark 10:13-16).

How often we in the church are like the disciples! We are ready to stop the children and keep them away. We say, "Wouldn't they be happier or better off in a room by themselves?" In reality we may be saying, "Those children will disturb our adult worship."

Let's look at some ways in which children and adults can become partners in worship.

Children Need a Sense of Belonging

We begin with an autobiographical point. I (D-B) grew up in a church where there was no such thing as an extended session. I participated in worship with my family. Some of my warmest memories are of worship, when I would get up and move from my parents to my grandmother, who was sitting on the other side of the sanctuary with her Sunday school class. Along the way, other members of the church helped me, touched me, smiled at me and talked with me. The feeling that I still remember is "I have a place in this church! I belong!"

Children need to feel welcome in their church family. They need to feel that worship is a part of their lives and that they are part of worship, since worship is the center of the life of the church. Think about being a child on Thanksgiving. The table is set with the best china, the food is prepared, and all your relatives are gathered together. And then you, the child, are sent to another room to eat. You are left out of the celebration. Worship is our church-family celebration. ·

The pastor plays an important role in helping children feel that they belong in the worshiping community. The pastor can help the children feel welcome. He or she can bend down to talk with the children, knowing their names and something about each one of them. Names are especially important. When we are called by name, we feel that we are known and accepted. From the pulpit the pastor can recognize events that are important in the lives of children, such as acknowledging those on the school honor roll and those performing in recitals or participating in athletic events. All these experiences help the child to feel, "I belong in this church. This is my family! These are my friends!"

Recall your experiences as a child in worship. What did adults do that made you feel welcomed and accepted? What adult behaviors told you that you were not accepted?

Including Children in Worship

Children need to be a part of the corporate worship of the local church. Therefore we need to plan intentionally for the inclusion and involvement of children in worship. Children can participate in the worship service in many ways. They can participate by greeting at the door with adult members of their immediate family or extended church family. They can serve as ushers. They can read the Scriptures or lead a litany or the call to worship. They can compose prayers, the invocation, or the call to worship. Doing this together with adult church members can be a growing experience for all, as the adults share the purposes and traditions of the elements of worship with the children.

Children can be involved in the music of worship in several ways. During church school they can become acquainted with the music and the history of various hymns. They will then be familiar with the music and will be able to sing the hymns with understanding during the worship time. The children can write new words to traditional hymn melodies, sharing their expression of worship with adult members of the congregation. Children can teach songs that they know to the congregation. Many older children can be encouraged to use their musical talents as they share in worship.

Many churches have a portion of the worship service just for children. This may be called the "Children's Sermon." This is in quotes, for often the "Children's Sermon" is really for adults. How often we have heard adult worshipers say, "Pastor, I get so much out of your children's sermons!" Perhaps we can call this an "illustrated sermon." A story can be told or a photo or filmstrip shown. Perhaps there are laypersons who can do this and relate it to the sermon. The pastor would need to provide the topic and Scripture several weeks in advance. These techniques need not be reserved for the children's sermon, however. Children and adults alike could more easily understand sermons that include simple illustrations and concrete items.

Another way of involving children in worship is to have special worship bulletins for them. Someone in the congregation may develop written activities dealing with the theme and events of each worship service to help the children become involved as they listen, look, and feel some of the things that are happening. These activities might include crossword puzzles, dot-to-dot drawings, word hunts, open-ended questions, or drawings. Each item would ask the children to listen or look for a specific thing in the worship service.

How are children presently involved in the worship service of your church? Think of individual children. How might each participate?

Preparing for Partnership

We cannot expect children and adults to begin to worship comfortably together if this has not been a part of their experience. Both groups have needs that must be considered. Some understanding of what is going to happen needs to be shared with both the children and the adults.

To begin with, the pastor needs to help the adults understand and appreciate the place of children in worship. For many adults this will mean a major change in attitude toward both children and corporate worship. Such changes require time and a nonthreatening environment. The pastor and others involved in facilitating the changes must be affirming and accepting of those who are hesitant or negative. When they become involved in the process, those with reservations are more likely to be accepting of the children.

Adult churchgoers recognize their need to worship and to be in a worshiping community. For a partnership with children to work, adults must recognize that children also have this same need, the need to be part of a worshiping family. Adults need to value the worship experience for persons of all ages as children of God.

Adults may need some preparation in defining worship. They will have questions such as these: What are the basic components of worship? Why do we follow the order of worship as we do? What can we change, and how much, and still feel the security of traditional worship? How can we keep our traditions and still provide worship that is meaningful to children? Will we compromise the needs of adults by including children?

Adults will also have some concrete questions about children in the worship service which can be dealt with by groups such as the deacons, the elders, or the worship committee or in open forum for interested adults. Each congregation must deal with the questions of its members and reach decisions that fit the church body. Some possibilities are suggested here to answer questions that may be raised.

"Should the children remain throughout the entire worship service each week?" There are many possibilities in answer to this question. One Sunday the children might stay for the entire worship service. The next week, they might stay for only the first half or come in for the last part. This can depend on what is taking place during worship on any particular Sunday. The key is flexibility. Don't get stuck in doing the same thing week in and week out! Experiment!

"What about junior church?" Junior church is a way of saying that worship is important and children are important. It may have many positive points, but it does separate the children from the main body of the church at worship. There often is little or no transfer of learning from the junior church experience to worship. John Westerhoff writes, "Something important is missed when children do not share their experience with the total congregation."[1] Children and adults alike may be enriched by shared participation as partners in worship.

"What if the children disturb the adult worshipers?" Children will squirm and make noise and fall asleep. The disturbance of adult worshipers can be lessened in several ways. Adults can set the atmosphere of worship by their own behavior. In some churches the worship atmosphere is quiet and in others it is open and spontaneous. In either

[1] John H. Westerhoff III, ed., *Values for Tomorrow's Children* (New York: The Pilgrim Press, 1970), p. 77.

case children need to know what is appropriate and need to be helped by example. One way of providing an example is for a significant adult to sit with each child. This may or may not be the parent. The adult helps the child to understand and participate. This also gives the child a sense of belonging and importance. Adults selected for this guidance role need to be able to relate to children, and be prepared to answer questions.

What questions do you think your congregation needs to explore? What groups within the church should deal with these questions? How can you ensure that all adults have opportunity to be heard and considered?

Children also need to be prepared for worship. Some preparation can be done in the church school when teachers and pastors share what worship is and why we worship. Children can go to the sanctuary during church school time and discuss the symbols they see and the arrangement of the sanctuary. They can see the baptistry and the organ, sit in the choir loft, and stand at the pulpit. Many of the things they do in church school can be preparation for participation in worship. They can write prayers and litanies, learn new songs and hymns, and learn the meaning of the Lord's Prayer, the Doxology, and the Gloria Patri.

Parents have a role in preparing their children for worship. When attending worship is a regular part of family life, it has importance for the children. Parents may not feel qualified to answer some of the questions their children ask. There are several ways to assist parents. A periodic class or discussion group, possibly called "Our Children and Worship," could be offered. This could deal with questions children ask, as well as with the practices and policies of your church regarding children. A pamphlet outlining these concerns could be prepared and given to parents. Or the pastor or other person involved in the ministry with children could call on families with children for the purpose of answering questions and sharing matters of practice.

Worship as Learning

Worship is a learning experience. Not only can we learn to apply truths to our daily living, but we also can learn about worship itself. Adults may need answers to some of the questions asked by children. All elements of the worship service have a potential for teaching. In today's church we miss many of the learning experiences because we do many things from habit, without thinking. During worship the meaning of the various parts of worship can be discussed—why we stand or sit at various times, the place of Scripture, the order of worship, the arrangement of the sanctuary, the symbols in the windows and on the furnishings, and the meaning of flowers, candles, and the open Bible. We can share the history of the people of the worshiping community.

Many adults would benefit from the same educational experiences that we would hope for our children in relation to worship. We in the church have assumed that adults know these things. As we include the children as partners, we can also educate our adult congregation and renew the meaning and tradition in worship.

Church Rites:
A Recognition and
Affirmation of Partnership

Though we are many, we are one body in union with Christ, and we are all joined to each other as different parts of one body (Romans 12:5).

The major gathering of the Christian community is for worship. A part of worship is the celebration of rites, the traditional ceremonies or observances of the church. Many churches include children in worship, but struggle with the role of children in certain rites.

Dedication

The act of dedication of parents and child is a rite that has its roots deep in the Old Testament. In 1 Samuel 1:19-28 we read of Hannah bringing Samuel into the house of the Lord for blessing and commitment. In the act of dedication today, parents bring their child before the congregation and before God, promising to raise the child in the nurture and understanding of the Lord. This dedication is the recognition that God is truly the giver of life and so the life should be dedicated to God. In some traditions this act is represented by baptism or christening, but in the Baptist tradition it is seen, not as a sacrament, but as a voluntary act of the parents.

Dedication is a threefold rite. First, it is the dedication of the child, usually an infant, in thanksgiving to God for the life God has given.

Second, it is the commitment of the parents. The parents come, recognizing the responsibilities of parenthood. They know they have the responsibility to help the child grow in his or her relationship with God and in his or her personal faith journey. Parents are saying that they will do everything they can to lead the child to Christian discipleship. Therefore it is important that at least one parent be an active Christian leading a responsible Christian life. To perform an act of dedication when parents are not Christian or are not active in their faith does not serve the purpose of dedication.

Third, dedication is also an act of commitment by the congregation. This congregational commitment can be kept only when parents live in the community where the rite takes place. Then the congregation can assist and support the parents with their task of raising their child in the Christian faith. The congregation can assume the important responsibility to provide a place for Christian growth and instruction, to provide an environment of acceptance and love, to provide resources for growth, and to provide a place for Christian commitment and service.

Dedication is the first sign of acceptance of the child by the church. Though the child will not remember this act, it is important for parents to remind the child of the day he or she was brought before the Lord. The members of the congregation also have a responsibility to remember this important day and their promise before God to encourage, support, and train the child in the Christian faith. Therefore, the congregation has an important responsibility to encourage parents who fall away from active participation, to remind the parents of the pledge they made, and to encourage their full participation in the life of the community of faith.

If dedication is this important, it cannot be placed outside the act of worship. Dedication of parents and child should be an integral part of worship and celebration of the faith. The Sunday of dedication is a Sunday when all of the children should be participating in worship. It is a time for those who have been dedicated in the past to be reminded by the pastor, parents, and friends that the church loves them and welcomed them in the same very special way. It is a time for members of the congregation to remember their pledge to all parents and children of the congregation.

Some ways of making dedication special follow:

- Provide sponsors for each dedication. Some churches have gotten away from the tradition of having persons stand up with the parents as witnesses to this important act. Perhaps it is time that this tradition be resumed in the free church. Two deacons or a couple (church-member friends of the parents) may serve as sponsors for the child. This couple can encourage and support the parents. They can serve as significant adults in the life of the child and in his or her spiritual journey.

- Develop a special litany for each child being dedicated.
- Have the whole family gather with the child (brothers, sisters, grandparents, aunts, uncles, and cousins) in front of the congregation to make it a special time of celebration and support for the family.
- Give each family a special gift representing this important day.
- Have a family member participate by assisting in worship.
- Have a special Scripture/poem/reading for each family.

Dedication is possibly the first step in the recognition and the affirmation that the child is an important person within the life of the church, this part of God's community. Dedication is a way of saying, "You are special! You are a child of God! You are an important part of this church family! We love you!"

Presentation of Bibles

Many churches present Bibles to their children as they enter third or fourth grade. This act or rite says several important things to the children receiving Bibles. It says that the church recognizes that the children are growing and maturing and now can read and study the Bible. The church is saying that it wants the children to read the Bible for themselves and to know its message and story.

This act also says that the Bible is an important book that is central to our life and our faith. When we present a Bible to a child, we are saying that the child has a responsibility to use the book. The church says that through the Bible and its study, we grow in the understanding of God's message for each of us. Through Bible study we come to a fuller understanding of Jesus Christ and his meaning for each of us so that we can move to a future commitment to Jesus Christ through his church.

The presentation of Bibles is a very special time. It needs to be done within the context of worship when the whole congregation can take part in affirming the children and the importance of the Bible in their lives.

Some suggestions to make this presentation of Bibles a special time are:

- As the Bible is presented to each child, have a layperson relate what the Bible means to him or her. This could be one of the child's sponsors, a church school teacher, a parent, or another significant adult known by the child. Each child would have one adult briefly explain how the Bible is important in his or her Christian life.

- Share with the children and the congregation about persons who have made great sacrifices in order that we might have this book today. The Bible should not be treated lightly.
- Following worship have a time of fellowship to honor those receiving Bibles. Some churches invite members of the congregation to sign the Bibles with a meaningful Scripture.
- As the Bibles are presented, the pastor or layperson could share a special biblical story or passage with each child, thus making it his or her own passage.
- In the following weeks invite the children to read the Scripture in worship.

The presentation of Bibles is somewhat of a "rite of passage" because the church is saying to the child, "We love you and we give you this very special book. It is not just a gift, but it is also a symbol of our belief that you are becoming able to understand what the Bible contains. We want the story and the message to become your story as you continue to grow in your faith journey."

Baptism

Baptism in our Baptist heritage is the outward sign of the inner commitment one makes to Jesus Christ as personal Lord and Savior. It should be a conscious choice by the individual being baptized. Baptism is also a renewal experience for others within the congregation who have been baptized, and it is a witness to those who are still at the point of making a decision.

Often churches raise this question: "What age should one be before he or she is baptized?" Baptists believe in the age of accountability. This means that the person is old enough to make the decision to be baptized without pressure and can understand what the commitment means. But what is the age of accountability? Is it the same for all persons?

The age of accountability may vary from person to person. Believer's baptism should occur when a person is developmentally able to have a new moral awareness and the capacity to renounce his or her sinful nature. The person, when baptized, takes on the responsibilities of a new life in Christ as a lifetime commitment. Since baptism requires a lifetime commitment and is a symbol of an abstract concept, it is very difficult for children to comprehend its significance. The ability to understand symbols and abstract concepts usually only begins to develop in late childhood.

Most churches have not struggled with the important question of children and baptism. Each church needs to deal with the questions surrounding children and baptism and then set its guidelines for baptism. What might some of these guidelines be?

- The church will encourage baptism only for persons older than a stated age. Persons coming forward prior to that age will be affirmed and celebrated by the congregation. The decision is important and it will not be taken lightly.
- The church will encourage persons to attend a pastor's class prior to baptism and for several weeks following baptism.
- The church will encourage baptism only for persons who are active in the life of the fellowship. Regular participation in worship and church school should be encouraged as part of the nurturing experience following baptism.

Some questions may be raised about whether age means maturity and understanding. When persons reach eighteen, do they automatically have more maturity than a twelve-year-old? No, we would agree that when a person becomes eighteen he or she does not automatically become an adult, but we are talking from the historical practice of the church and the baptism of adults.

To use a personal experience; I (D-B) was baptized at age twelve along with my classmates in the First Baptist Church of Santa Ana, California. We had all participated in a pastor's class and, in the "eyes of the church," were ready for baptism. But I did not understand the meaning of baptism until years later in my young adulthood. At twelve I was doing something important and special but without full meaning or understanding of what it meant in my life!

Would it have been better if I had waited until age eighteen or twenty-one? No one can say, but what we *are* saying is that each church needs to deal seriously with the whole question of baptism. Each church needs to set standards and criteria by which that church can live and function and help children, youth, and adults understand the importance of baptism. Baptism is related to repentance and faith. Historically Baptists have practiced believer's baptism, which symbolizes that one has repented, and on faith have yielded themselves to God.

Richard Waltz writes,

> At times we scoff at those who practice infant baptism and require catechism classes, but is what we are doing any better? If children are expected to be responsible for this all-important decision in their lives, how much

more ought we be willing to work patiently with them until they can make a meaningful decision?[1]

Here are some suggestions for making baptism a special time for the participants and the congregation, no matter at what age baptism occurs.

- Have the pastor's class write a litany on what baptism means to them. Use this litany in the congregational worship service.
- Put a short biography of each candidate in the bulletin.
- Give each candidate a special gift, such as a plaque, a book, or a special symbol.
- Sing a verse or two of each candidate's favorite hymn while he or she is in the baptistry.
- Have a sponsor or deacon enter the water with the candidate to show that this person is becoming the spiritual guide for the Christian growth of the baptismal candidate for the year to come.
- Have a celebration meal following baptism when the "family of God" can break bread together.
- Have a layperson or a member of the candidate's family give a testimony about what baptism has meant in his or her personal life.

Baptism is a special time. It needs to be presented, not as a completion, but as the beginning. It represents only the first few steps in the process of Christian growth. In many of our churches, time is given to preparation for the act of baptism, but as soon as the child, youth, or adult leaves the water, each is left on his or her own to grow or die in the Christian life. We need to develop ways to support and encourage growth!

Baptism needs to be a celebration when the congregation says to the person being baptized, "We love you. We rejoice with you. We will support you, encourage you, and challenge you. This is not the end of your spiritual journey. We expect you to continue to grow!" Children need to be part of the affirming congregation in this celebration.

Church Membership

Church membership and baptism are tied together. Baptism is the symbol of the personal commitment of one's life. Church membership is the joining of a person to a church family and their covenanting together to work for the purpose of the church and to support its mission.

As with baptism, we believe churches have to decide when children should become members and what criteria to use in bringing persons into membership. We have a real concern for churches that accept children as members but do not allow them to function as members.

[1]Richard L. Waltz, "Children and Decision," *Baptist Leader* (June 1979), p. 54.

We believe that churches need to encourage child members to participate as partners in the total life of the church according to their ability to serve.

> There are different ways of serving, but the same Lord is served. There are different abilities to perform service, but the same God gives ability to everyone for their particular service (1 Corinthians 12:5-6).

If children are members, then they are members in the fullest sense. We need to listen and seriously consider their ideas and concerns.

What does it mean to be a member of your church? Which membership functions are open to children and which are not? Are all members encouraged to participate in some aspect of church life? What does the church teach about membership if one cannot function as a member for a number of years after joining the church?

If we honestly consider membership rights and responsibilities to be for all members, then children who are members must be included. This inclusion will mean recognizing and affirming that we are in partnership in ministry and that Christian witness and responsibility are for both adults and children. We can affirm that these are for all who follow Jesus Christ. We believe that the church needs to be looking for ways to involve all its members, not in a junior capacity but in full-fledged membership!

Lord's Supper

On Sunday morning we gather for congregational worship to express praise and thanksgiving to God. Many churches want children present for part or all of the service, not only as observers but also as participants. Children too are part of the community of faith. It is important for the child's educational process and the child's nurturing in the Christian faith to include everyone in this aspect of church life.

While churches may provide an inclusive atmosphere for children, they still may not know what to do with them during the Lord's Supper. Churches need to deal with the question of children and their participation in the Lord's Supper.

What is the custom of children and the Lord's Supper in your church? Recall being a child in worship. Were you included or not included in the Lord's Supper? How did you feel? In Deuteronomy 6:4-9 we are told that we must teach our children. If they are not allowed to participate in the meal, what are we saying to them? What is the message received by a child who hears the minister say, "This table is open to all," and yet he or she is not allowed to partake?

In the Jewish tradition, children have a very important part in the Passover meal. The children partake of the meal with the adults and they participate in the remembrance by asking the important question: "Why do we do this?" The children in our churches may be asking the similar questions: "Why do we eat this bread? Why do we drink this juice?" These questions could be asked by children as part of the Communion service, with the pastor responding in words that the children would understand.

Children need to be told the meaning of the Lord's Supper. This could be done through a visit by the pastor to the primary, middler, and junior classes to share the meaning of the Lord's Supper with the children. The children could then partake of the elements during the worship service as part of the total church family. Children should later be encouraged to respond, in their own words, telling what the Lord's Supper means to them.

It is helpful to have some laypeople aware of children who are in worship without adult supervision. These adults can sit by the children, "adopting" them. The adults can explain what is going on during the Communion service.

The Lord's Supper or Communion can be a very special event for the life of the church and for the children involved. It is a way of truly feeling a part of the fellowship and being affirmed as a person.

Some churches, when dealing with the question of whether children should participate in the Lord's Supper, may feel more comfortable with the traditional stance of many American Baptist Churches. This stance is that the ordinance of baptism admits a person to the Lord's Supper.

Churches who view the Lord's Supper in this way should still make an intentional effort to share the meaning of this event with children. As partners in ministry with children, adults have a responsibility to listen to children's questions, feelings, and concerns about waiting until baptism in order to participate.

The board of deacons, pastor, parents, and members of the congregation need to set standards for children's participation in the Lord's Supper. Whether these standards include involving children in this rite or postponing their involvement until after baptism, the church's struggle needs to include finding a way to help children feel a part of the community of faith during this significant event.

Partners in Mission

"Go therefore and make disciples of all nations, baptizing them in the name of the Father and of the Son and of the Holy Spirit, teaching them to observe all that I have commanded you..." (Matthew 28:19-20, RSV).

"The Spirit of the Lord is upon me,
because he has anointed me to preach good news to the poor.
He has sent me to proclaim release to the captives
and recovering of sight to the blind,
to set at liberty those who are oppressed,
to proclaim the acceptable year of the Lord."
—Luke 4:18-19(RSV)

Defining Our Mission

The church is involved in mission but is often confused about what that mission is. Interviews with children have shown that they do not easily understand the concept of mission. They can understand the more concrete terms associated with mission. They understand that a missionary is a person who is sent to tell others about Jesus. They understand that a mission field is an area where missionaries work. They understand that the church sends money to help support missionaries. Some children can identify Paul as a missionary.

The concept of mission as expressed by Jesus in Matthew 28:19-20 and Luke 4:18-19 includes not only sending missionaries and supporting them in mission but also becoming personally and individually involved with persons in physical and spiritual need. Mission is not done only within the walls of the church. It also means going out on special work or service.

What does mission mean to you? How are you involved in mission? What is the mission of your local church? What is your personal mission?

Developing Attitudes Toward Mission

Children will develop attitudes about mission as adults assist them in building their self-esteem. Children can look outside themselves to give and share only when they feel loved and competent. They will most likely develop the attitudes that are shown to them and the ones they observe adults showing to one another within the congregation.

What are the attitudes that you would like to have children develop toward mission? Do these reflect your own attitudes? Are they in harmony with the attitudes of the congregation?

Children must see adults giving time and money to mission. If we want children to feel that mission is the main activity and responsibility of the church, they must see the church spending much of its time and money on mission. If we want them to see mission as exciting, they must be associated with adults who reflect excitement for their mission involvement. To develop attitudes of concern for mission, children must be in an environment of mission concern in which the whole church takes mission seriously, reaching out to the community as well as supporting missions far away.

Children will have positive attitudes toward mission if their own efforts are accepted and encouraged. The child who invites a friend to church will learn the value of individual mission if the friend is accepted by adult church members. Children will develop positive attitudes toward mission if they are supported when they need sponsors for the CROP Walk or donations for UNICEF. Children's attitudes toward mission will be influenced by the kind of support they receive when they are involved in mission.

Learning About Mission

Many local church or area missions committees hold annual mission fairs or schools of mission. Children can be included as partners in these mission learning events. Children are interested in how people live in other parts of the world. Films, filmstrips, and well-told stories of mission fields will be interesting to children and help them to understand the difference missions can make in people's lives. Mission speakers who will answer children's questions and who have things from the mission field for children to touch, taste, and explore can spark a lifelong interest in missions.

Mission information included during worship will reach adults and children alike. It will also emphasize that mission is not a separate activity but an integral part of the life of the church and that all persons and all activities are involved in mission. Sharing the local mission of the church during worship will keep all informed and give importance to the role of the local church in the community.

Even though there may not be as much mission information as they would like included in curriculum materials, church school teachers can include additional mission education in their sessions with children. The teacher can use church school time to reflect on mission activities that the children and teacher have been involved in together. The teacher can help expand the children's concept of mission by identifying service activities as part of the mission of the church. The teacher can help children to consider what their individual mission might be and encourage them in their mission efforts.

Doing Mission as Partners

Children learn best by doing and reflecting. They will learn about mission and develop positive attitudes toward mission as they are involved in doing mission. They will come to understand mission as they discuss their experiences and what these experiences mean with adults who are involved in doing mission with them.

There are many ways in which children and adults can participate as partners in mission efforts. First, part of mission is the financial support of those on the mission field. Children can earn money for various mission projects by working on a recycling program. Newspapers and aluminum cans can be collected and turned in for cash. Adults may need to help by saving cans or newspapers for the children to collect and by helping them deliver them to a recycling center. These experiences are most meaningful when adults and children participate together.

Children can be involved in local mission. If the church has a mission of feeding people who are hungry, children can help sort canned goods or organize the food pantry shelves. If the church has a mission to shut-ins, children can participate by being in an adopt-a-grandparent program or by sending birthday and holiday cards to shut-ins or by visiting shut-ins who are alone. If the church has a ministry to refugees, the children can help welcome the families, become friends with the new children, and help both family and children become acquainted with their new community.

Children can be involved in national and international mission by writing letters to missionaries. They must understand, though, that the missionaries may not be able to answer. Children will need to see that the missionary will appreciate knowing that they are supported and encouraged by the children. The names, addresses, and birthdays of missionaries and their families are available through your mission support person.

What missions of your church currently involve children? In what ways could they be involved?

Partnership in mission with children will take time and effort, training for adults and children, an increased awareness of what the church's mission is, and adults who will accept responsibility for being examples of people who live out mission. Partnership in mission will also require pastors who are interested in mission and in children and who can see the possibility of their being involved in mission. Partnership will take effort from the adult members of the congregation.

How can your church begin to establish a partnership between adults and children for mission? Here are some suggestions. First, mission must be defined by the local congregation. Each local church must decide its own involvement in mission, what it means, and where children can be involved. Second, adults must be educated for partnership, understanding that children learn best by participation, involvement, and seeing action modeled. Third, adults and children alike need to be informed about mission and what mission is and what is happening internationally, nationally, locally, and personally. Fourth, the church, individually and corporately, must be active in doing mission!

Adults as
Advocates for Children

And look out for one another's interests, not just for your own. The attitude
you should have is the one that Christ Jesus had (Phillippians 2:4-5).

Who Speaks Out for the Children in Your Church?

- Who speaks out when the budget is made and Christian education
  and children's ministry is determined?
- Who speaks out when the children are overlooked during potluck
  dinners or Bible-study times?
- Who speaks out when the children are all treated the same without
  regard for age or size?
- Who speaks out for the children who are restless sitting on the
  hard pews during worship?

Who Speaks Out for the Children in Your Community?

- Who speaks out for the children whose parents leave them at the
  day care center at 7 A.M. and pick them up at 7 P.M.?
- Who speaks out for the children of families divided by divorce or
  death or separation?
- Who speaks out for the children who are physically, mentally, or
  sexually abused?

- Who speaks out for the children who are living in a new environment and who cannot communicate in English?

Who Speaks Out for the Children of the World?

- Who speaks out for the children who are worried about nuclear war or disaster?
- Who speaks out for the children of the future for whom toxic wastes and contaminants in the water are bringing the possibilities of birth defects or sterility?
- Who speaks out for the children caught in the middle of economic depression?
- Who speaks out for the children who are starving?
- Who speaks out for children who must live in the midst of violent political upheaval and bloodshed?
- Who speaks out for the children who have never heard of Jesus Christ?

Who Speaks Out for the Children?

Who speaks out for the children? Persons who believe in children, who believe that the future is now and that the children are our hope. Persons who believe that children need to know about God's love. Persons who value children's excitement, their anticipation, their many questions, and their joy in the newness of life.

Who speaks for the children? It is hoped that you and I will do so—those of us who are involved in working with children. We need to see our role as advocates of children. According to Webster, an advocate is one who "pleads the cause of another." We need to plead the cause of children. When the world, the community, and the church will not listen to them, we need to speak out in support of children and their needs.

How Do We Speak Out for Children?

How can we make our voices heard? How can we know the issues and facts concerning children in the world?

How Can We Speak Out for Children in the Church

- Serve on boards and committees making decisions that affect children.
- Learn what your denomination has set as priorities for children.
- Learn what your denomination is doing for children.
- Begin an adult Bible-study group to consider the roles of children in the Bible. Affirm the value of children and examine your own responses.

- Educate the members of your congregation. Make available lists of institutions and organizations that serve children and that need financial aid.
- Encourage your church and its members to increase their financial support for groups speaking for children.
- Join with children in your church in planning and carrying out projects such as:
    —planting and caring for a vegetable garden and sharing the produce with those in need.
    —earning money to help children in need by having bake sales, recycling projects, car washes.
    —forming an intergenerational church school class.

How Can We Speak Out for Children in Our Community?

- Begin a study group to learn about the needs of children in your community and the services that are currently available.
- Adopt a child who needs a home.
- Open your home to foster children.
- Volunteer to serve on an abuse hotline or in a shelter for battered women and their children.
- Survey the space, resources, and people of your church to determine whether there might be new ways of serving children in the community, especially those in need of care, food, clothing, or shelter.
- Volunteer to be with children in such programs as child care, after school programs, tutoring, health clinics, and hot-breakfast programs.

How Can We Speak Out for the Children in Our Nation and the World?

- Keep informed about legislation that affects children.
- Write or call your congressional representative, your senator, your state representatives, and the governor.
- Encourage others to write to support or disagree with specific legislation, supplying them with the addresses and necessary information.
- Urge your denomination and your city and state ecumenical or interfaith bodies to be advocates for children.
- Pray regularly for children.
- Support children when they need sponsors for programs or other projects that children do to help raise money for children of the world.

Your voice will count. You can make a difference for children in your church, in your community, and in the world!

Then he took a child and had him stand in front of them. He put his arms around him and said to them, "Whoever welcomes in my name one of these children, welcomes me; and whoever welcomes me, welcomes not only me but also the one who sent me" (Mark 9:36-37).

Bibliography

For Bible Study

Bringing Up Children in the Christian Faith, by John H. Westerhoff III. San Francisco: Harper San Francisco, 1984. Parents will find many practical suggestions on praying, celebrating, listening and talking, telling Bible stories, and performing acts of service and witness with their children.

Experiencing the Bible with Children, by Dorothy J. Furnish. Nashville: Abingdon Press, 1990. A resource for both parents and teachers to help children understand and experience the Bible in creative ways.

Let the Children Come: A New Approach to Children's Sermons, by Brent D. Baker. Minneapolis: Augsburg Fortress, 1991. Children's sermons that have been used to help children understand Christianity by helping them experience Christianity.

Teaching the Bible to Elementary Children, by Dick Murray. Nashville: Discipleship Resources, 1990. Presents ways to teach the Bible to younger children to help them know God.

On Children

Believers' Baptism for Children of the Church, by Marlin Jeschke. Scottdale, Pa.: Herald Press, 1983. The author gives his theology of believers' baptism for children of the church.

Black Children: Their Roots, Culture, and Learning Styles, revised edition, by Janice E. Hale-Benson. Baltimore: The Johns Hopkins University Press, 1986. Advocates that education of black children be approached from an awareness that their unique culture plays a significant role in learning. This is based on her extensive research and on numerous reviews of literature from many fields.

Child Sexual Abuse: A Handbook for Clergy and Church Members, by Lee W. Carlson. Valley Forge: Judson Press, 1988. How churches can respond to the victims of child sexual abuse, the offenders, and their families.

Children, Children! A Ministry Without Boundaries, by Dorlis Brown Glass. Nashville: General Board of Discipleship, United Methodist Church, 1986.

Children in the Worshipping Community, by David Ng and Virginia Thomas. Atlanta: John Knox Press, 1981. A resourceful book inviting congregations to understand children and learn to include them in the total life of the church. 61

Faith Development in Early Childhood, edited by Dolores A. Blazer. Kansas City, Mo.: Sheed and Ward, 1989. Key essays from a Kanuga National Symposium dealing with (1) the process by which young children form religious faith in their first years and (2) given this, what the church can do to support the process.

Handbook of Preschool Religious Education, edited by Donald Ratcliff. Birmingham, Ala.: Religious Education Press, 1989. A comprehensive resource on religious and moral development of preschool children; it contains a section focusing on methodology and an evaluation of religious education for preschoolers.

The Hurried Child: Growing up Too Fast Too Soon, by David Elkind. Reading, Mass.: Addison-Wesley Publishing Co., Inc., 1988. The book takes a hard look at children and stress. It explores the unique burdens we have brought upon our children and offers insights, advice, and hope for solving these problems.

Precious in His Sight: A Guide to Child Advocacy, by Diana Garland. Birmingham, Ala.: Hew Hope, 1993. A resource that identifies children and families that are failing in our nation. It suggests ways to become advocates of justice for children, especially those with the greatest needs, and it explores the place of children in our churches.

The Spiritual Life of Children, by Robert Coles. Boston: Houghton Mifflin Co., 1990. Numerous candid responses from children, through interviews and drawings, related to their religious and spiritual lives—Christian, Jewish, and Islamic.

Your Child's Self-Esteem: The Key to His Life, by Dorothy C. Briggs. New York: Doubleday and Co., Inc., 1975. A number of step-by-step guidelines for raising children are provided in this helpful book. The author has an especially helpful section on discipline.

On Teaching and Learning

Building a Great Children's Ministry, by Evelyn M. R. Johnson and Bobbie Bower. Nashville: Abingdon Press, 1992. The authors offer specific suggestions to churches on how to plan for children's ministries. Worksheets and questionnaires are included.

Teaching Young Children: A Guide for Teachers and Leaders, by MaryJane Pierce Norton. Nashville: Discipleship Resources, 1989. The central theme in this book is the importance of keeping the needs of the child foremost. Practical teaching tips are offered;

equipment and materials for each age level are listed; and plans for teaching are included.

Working with Elementary Children: A Guide for Teachers and Leaders, by Lois M. Runk. Nashville: Discipleship Resources, 1988. An easy-to-use resource for teachers as they plan church school sessions. Includes outlines of developmental characteristics of children, tips on creating an inviting teaching area, and insights into the ministry of the teacher.

Program Resources

Building a New Community: God's Children Overcoming Racism, for teacher and student. Nashville: Cokesbury, 1992. A thirteen-session curriculum resource for older elementary and/or middle school children, prepared by the General Board of Discipleship, Division of Church School Publications, The United Methodist Church.

Helping Kids Care: Harmony-Building Activities for Home, Church and School, by Camy Condon and James McGinnis. Bloomington, Ind.: Meyer-Stone Books, 1988. A practical resource with many illustrations related to peacemaking, global concerns, issues of aging, and awareness of persons with disabilities. For use with children ages eight to twelve.

My Life: A Steward's Life, by Barbara Fillette. Grandville, Mich.: Reformed Church Press, 1992. A broadly graded stewardship-education resource to use with children preschool (age four) through grade two and with children in grades three through six. Five sessions incorporating a wide variety of activities.

Peace Works: Young Peacemakers Project Book II, by Kathleen Fry-Miller and Judith Myers-Walls. Elgin, Ill.: Brethren Press, 1989. Numerous activities on everyday peacemaking for children ages three to ten. Useful for families as well as children's leaders.

Self-Esteem: A Classroom Affair—101 Ways to Help Children Like Themselves, Vol. 1 and Vol. 2, by Michele and Craig Borba. San Francisco: Harper San Francisco, Vol. 1, 1984; Vol. 2, 1985. Activities and ideas to help create an atmosphere in which children learn to like themselves. All have been child tested.

Young Peacemakers' Project Book, by Kathleen Fry-Miller and Judith Myers-Walls. Elgin, Ill.: Brethren Press, 1988. Fun and creative peacemaking projects for educating preschool through elementary-age children.

Additional Resources
Published by Judson Press

Basic Teacher Skills, by Richard E. Rusbuldt. 0-8170-0919-1

Child Sexual Abuse: A Handbook for Clergy and Church Members, by Lee W. Carlson. 0-8170-1133-1

Children Together, Volume 2, edited by Elizabeth Wright Gale. 0-8170-0974-4

Children Together, Volume 3, edited by Gracie R. McCay and Virginia A. Sargent. 0-8170-1078-5

Children's Time in Worship, by Arline J. Ban. 0-8170-0902-7

Christian Education in the Small Church, by Donald L. Griggs and Judy McKay Walther. 0-8170-1103-X

Church Family Gatherings, edited by Joe Leonard, Jr. 0-8170-0809-8

A Growing Church School, by Kenneth D. Blazier. 0-8170-0785-7

Learning Centers for Better Christian Education, by Rachel Gillespie Lee. 0-8170-0927-2

Planning for Teaching Church School, by Donald L. Griggs. 0-8170-1079-3

Ready, Set . . . Sing!—Songs for Sunday and Every Day, edited by Mary M. Nicol and Pamela K. Roth. 0-8170-1155-2

Teach Me to Teach, by Dorothy G. Swain. 0-8170-0316-9